DUDLEY SCHOOLS
LIBRARY SERVICE

KU-337-516

Schools Library and Information Services

S00000748048

Instruments and Music

Daniel Nunn

www.raintreepublishers.co.uk
Visit our website to find out
more information about
Raintree books.

To order:

☎ Phone 0845 6044371

🗎 Fax +44 (0) 1865 312263

🖥 Email myorders@raintreepublishers.co.uk

Customers from outside the UK please telephone +44 1865 312262

Raintree is an imprint of Capstone Global Library Limited, a company incorporated in England and Wales having its registered office at 7 Pilgrim Street, London, EC4V 6LB – Registered company number: 6695582

Text © Capstone Global Library Limited 2012
First published in hardback in 2012
The moral rights of the proprietor have been asserted.

All rights reserved. No part of this publication may be reproduced in any form or by any means (including photocopying or storing it in any medium by electronic means and whether or not transiently or incidentally to some other use of this publication) without the written permission of the copyright owner, except in accordance with the provisions of the Copyright, Designs and Patents Act 1988 or under the terms of a licence issued by the Copyright Licensing Agency, Saffron House, 6–10 Kirby Street, London EC1N 8TS (www.cla.co.uk). Applications for the copyright owner's written permission should be addressed to the publisher.

Edited by Daniel Nunn, Rebecca Rissman, and Harriet Milles
Designed by Joanna Hinton-Malivoire
Picture research by Mica Brancic
Originated by Capstone Global Library Ltd.
Production by Eirian Griffiths
Printed and bound in China by Leo Paper Products Ltd

ISBN 978 1 406 22993 6 (hardback)
15 14 13 12 11
10 9 8 7 6 5 4 3 2 1

British Library Cataloguing in Publication Data
Nunn, Daniel.
 Instruments and Music – (Acorn plus)
 1. Musical instruments–Pictorial works–Juvenile literature.
 I. Title II. Series
 784.1'9-dc22
A full catalogue record for this book is available from the British Library.

Acknowledgements
We would like to thank the following for permission to reproduce photographs: Alamy **pp. 9 left** (© OnTheRoad), **11 right** (© Robert Fried), **13 middle** (© Tom Carter); Getty Images **p. 13 right** (Taxi/Simon Watson); iStockphoto **p. 6, 22 tuba** (© Rodrigo Blanco); Photolibrary **pp. 7** (Image Source), **8** (Jupiterimages/Pixland); Shutterstock **pp. 4** (© wavebreakmedia ltd), **5 left** (© Lowe Llaguno), **5 top right, 10, 22 clarinet** (© Olly), **5 bottom right** (© gosn.Momcilo), **6 harp** (© Dmitry Skutin), **6 tuba** (© grublee), **6 clarinet** (© Mikeledray), **6 keyboards** (© Nikita Rogul), **6 violin, 22 violin** (© Timmary), **9 right** (© Mountainpix), **11 left** (© Ben Smith), **12, 22 piano** (© Karma Shuford), **13 left** (© Katrina Leigh), **14** (© Kazberry), **15 left** (© Petrenko Andriy), **15 right** (© Nicholas Sutcliffe), **16** (© Testing), **18** (© Mary416), **19** (© Oleg Kirillov), **20** (© Filipe B. Varela), **21** (© Ferenc Szelepcsenyi), **22 marimba**, 17 (© Jorge R. Gonzalez).

Front cover photograph of a Cuban band playing in a street in Cuba reproduced with permission of Photolibrary/Age Fotostock (Angelo Cavalli). Back cover of marimbas players reproduced with permission of Shutterstock (© Jorge R. Gonzalez).

We would like to thank Jennifer Johnson for her invaluable help in the preparation of this book.

Every effort has been made to contact copyright holders of any material reproduced in this book. Any omissions will be rectified in subsequent printings if notice is given to the publisher.

DUDLEY PUBLIC LIBRARIES

L

748048   Sch

J 785

Contents

Some words appear in bold, **like this**. You can find out what they mean in "Words to know" on page 23.

Music all around us

There are many different types of music. Some people like **pop** music. Some people like **classical** music. Some people like **jazz** music. Some people like **folk** music.

You can listen to music in the street. You can listen to music on the beach. You can listen to music at a concert. Music is all around us.

Musical instruments

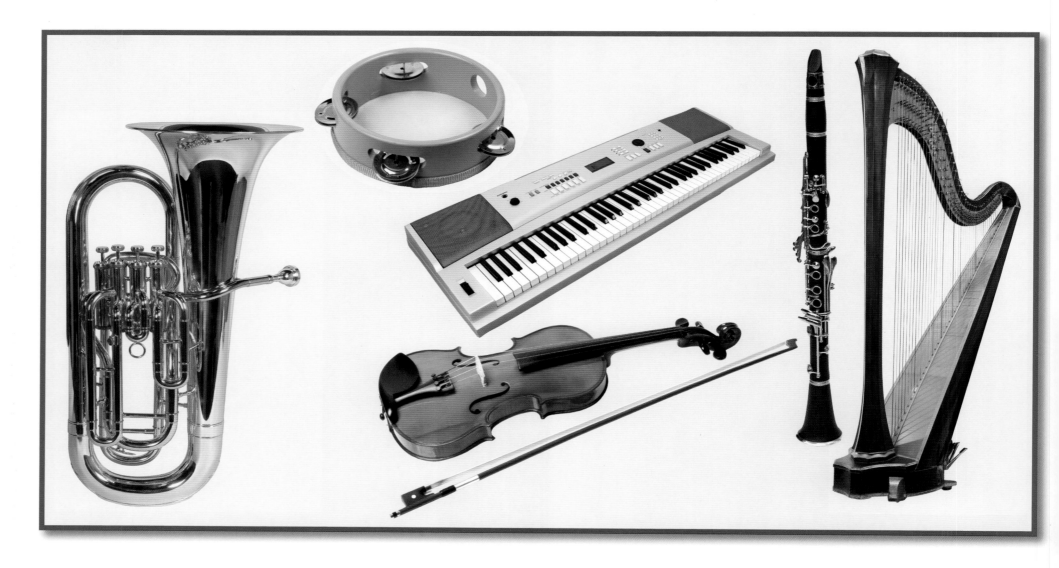

People use musical instruments to make music. There are lots of different types of musical instruments. They all make different sounds.

Some instruments play loud sounds. Some instruments play quiet sounds. Some instruments play high **notes**. Some instruments play low notes. Some instruments are used to keep **rhythm**.

Brass instruments

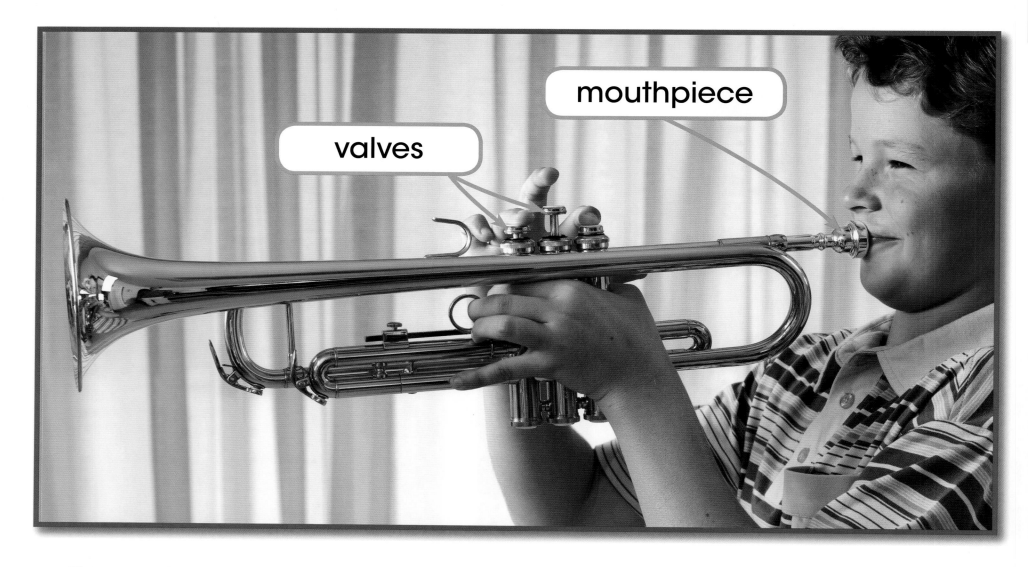

mouthpiece

valves

Brass instruments are instruments you blow. You make a sound by making your lips buzz into a **mouthpiece**. You play different **notes** by pressing keys called **valves**.

sousaphone

alphorn

Trumpets, sousaphones, and trombones are all brass instruments. An alphorn is a brass instrument – even though it is made of wood! It is a brass instrument because you make a sound by buzzing your lips.

Woodwind instruments

keys

Woodwind instruments are also instruments you blow. Like brass instruments, you make a sound by blowing into a **mouthpiece**. You play different **notes** by covering holes or pressing keys.

reed

pan pipes

Clarinets, oboes, and saxophones make a sound when you blow against a **reed**. Flutes and pan pipes don't have reeds. They make a sound when you blow against the edge of a hole.

Keyboard instruments

keys

Keyboard instruments have lots of keys to press.

You play different **notes** by pressing different keys.

Keyboard instruments make sounds in different ways.

strings

hammer

pipes

accordion

Pianos have hammers inside that hit strings when you press the keys. Pipe organs make sounds by pushing air through pipes. Accordions make sounds when you squeeze air through them.

String instruments

string

String instruments have strings stretched across them. Guitars, violins, cellos, and harps are all string instruments.

bow

You make a sound by touching the strings. Some string instruments you **pluck** with your fingers. Some string instruments you play with a **bow**.

Percussion instruments

Percussion instruments are instruments you beat, shake, or rub. Some percussion instruments are used to keep **rhythm**. Some percussion instruments can play a **tune**.

mallet

marimba

You play some percussion instruments with mallets or sticks. You play other percussion instruments with your hands or fingers. Drums, cymbals, tambourines, and marimbas are all percussion instruments.

Voices

You can make music with your voice, too. This is called singing. There are lots of different styles of singing.

You can make other types of music without instruments, too. You can **hum** a **tune** with your mouth closed. You can **whistle** a tune by blowing through your teeth and lips.

All together

Every instrument has its own sound. We can make music together by playing different instruments at the same time. A band is a group of a few people playing different instruments.

orchestra

An **orchestra** can have more than 100 players. Most orchestras have string instruments, brass instruments, woodwind instruments, and percussion instruments.

Can you remember?

Can you find the picture of a woodwind instrument? Which is a brass instrument? Can you see any keyboard or percussion instruments? Can you find a string instrument?

Answers on page 24

Words to know

bow stick with horsehairs stretched across it that is used to play some string instruments

classical type of music that was played a long time ago

folk music from a particular country or area

hum sing or make music with your mouth closed

jazz music in which the musicians change the notes as they play

mouthpiece part of an instrument that you blow into

note sound made by your voice, or by a musical instrument

orchestra large group of musicians playing together

pluck pull and let go strings on an instrument to make sounds

pop type of music that is modern and very popular

reed part of a woodwind instrument that moves when you blow it to make a sound

rhythm repeated pattern of sound

tune series of musical notes that sound nice together

valve key on a brass instrument that you press to change the note

whistle make a sound by blowing through your lips and teeth

Index

Answers to quiz on page 22:
a) percussion b) keyboard c) string d)woodwind e) brass

Notes for parents and teachers

After reading

Play some music to the class from the following selection.

Carnival of the Animals (Saint Saens)

Peter and the Wolf (Sergei Prokofiev)

The Young Person's Guide to the Orchestra (Benjamin Britten)

Help the children to identify the sounds of some of the instruments in this book.